IF NOT FOR WEATHER WE WOULD ALL BE NAKED!

By: Christopher Nance

Illustrated By: Ardavan and Khashayar Javid

First Edition

Printed in Singapore by Eurasia Press Pte Ltd

Published by Christopher Productions Inc.
CPI Publishers
10153 1/2 Riverside Drive, #266
Toluca Lake, CA 91602
(888) 831-9268

Nicholette Ortega Nance, Publisher
Paul Villar, Assistant
Stephen Garcia, Editor

ISBN 0-9648363-8-6
Library of Congress Catalog Card Number - 97-095323

Dr. Seuss, motivated me to read with his books. This book and all the crazy looking characters in it are dedicated to the man who made reading fun for me. To the wonderful memory of Dr. Seuss.

My new motivation is my God, My Wife Nicholette, my family and friends.

Special thanks to the people of Catalina Island. Avalon will always be my quiet writing place and spark that got this book started... and finished.

IF NOT FOR WEATHER, WE WOULD ALL BE NAKED.
THIS IS THE TRUTH, AND YOU JUST CAN'T FAKE IT.

IF NOT FOR THE STUFF THAT COMES OUT OF THE
SKY, WE WOULD ALL BE STANDING AROUND NAKED,
RED FACED AND SHY.

THE TROPOSPHERE IS WHERE ALL OUR WEATHER EXISTS. THIS STRETCH OF ATMOSPHERE HAS EVERYTHING ON THE LIST, FROM DUST STORMS TO TORNADOES, SNOW, SLEET AND HAIL.
THERE IS RAIN, SUN AND WIND TO BLOW THE SAILS.

THE TROPOSPHERE STRETCHES FROM THE OCEAN TO THE SKY, MORE THAN TEN THOUSAND FEET UP. HIGHER THAN BIRDS WANT TO FLY.

ABOVE THE TROPOSPHERE IS THE STRATOSPHERE, NOT A LOT OF WEATHER REALLY HAPPENS HERE.

NOW THAT YOU KNOW WHERE OUR WEATHER LIVES, LET ME, PLEASE LET ME TELL YOU WHAT WEATHER IS.

WEATHER IS RAIN, WIND, SUN AND HEAT. WEATHER MAKES GRASS GROW SO COWS HAVE FOOD TO EAT.

WEATHER FILLS OUR RIVERS, LAKES, OCEANS AND STREAMS. WEATHER MAKES IT POSSIBLE TO FLY KITES ON STRING.

WEATHER MAKES PLANTS GROW, LIKE GRASS AND TREES. TREES HELP MAKE OXYGEN FOR US TO BREATHE.

NOW, I AM A WAHBAH, AND A BEAUTIFUL ONE TOO.
WAHBAHS LIVE EVERYWHERE, EXCEPT IN THE ZOO.

I AM AFFECTED BY THE THINGS THAT ALSO AFFECT YOU, LIKE THE THICK FOG IN THE MORNING THAT'S HARD TO SEE THROUGH.

FOG IS PART OF THE WEATHER. FOG'S A LOW FLYING CLOUD. MILLIONS OF EVAPORATING WATER PARTICLES MAKE UP ITS SHROUD.

IF YOU WANT TO BE SEEN IN THE FOG, HERE'S WHAT YOU DO, DRESS IN VERY BRIGHT COLORS.
REFLECTORS HELP TOO.

IF YOU WANT TO SERVE YOUR FAMILY SNOW FOR DINNER. HERE IS A RECIPE THAT IS ALWAYS A WINNER.

START WITH ONE FAT RAIN CLOUD, THEN ADD SOME COLD AIR.
TAKE THE CLOUD UP TO THE MOUNTAINS, BUT WEAR YOUR LONG UNDERWEAR.

THE HIGHER YOU GO THE COLDER THE AIR GETS. WHEN THE AIR REACHES FREEZING, ADD THE RAIN CLOUD FOR KICKS.

ZAP, POW, BOOM, WHAT A LOVELY TUNE.
ZING, BONG, ZONG, IS MOTHER NATURE'S SONG.

WHAT HAPPENS NOW, YOU SHOULD KNOW. THE
FREEZING AIR TURNS THE RAIN
TO SNOW.

BUNDLE UP WARM, DINNER IS SERVED.
HAVING SNOW FOR DINNER... WOW! THAT TAKES
SOME NERVE.

WHEN YOU GET DOWN TO IT, WEATHER IS EVERYWHERE. WEATHER EFFECTS THE FOOD WE EAT, OUR CLOTHES AND OUR HAIR.

LET ME SHOW YOU WHAT I MEAN. LET ME SHOW YOU I SAY. YOU TURN THE PAGE AND I'LL WALK THIS WAY.

LET'S START WITH MY SHIRT. IT IS MADE OUT OF COTTON.

WHAT MAKES COTTON PLANTS GROW, OR HAVE YOU FORGOTTEN?

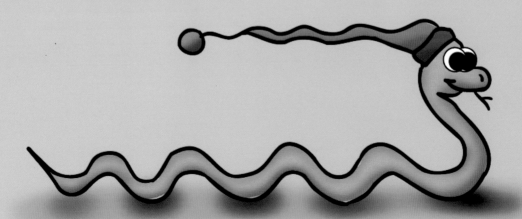

THE COTTON PLANTS NEED SUN, SOIL AND RAIN. THEN STAND BACK. WATCH OUT! WEATHER'S GOING TO DO ITS THING.

SLOWLY, VERY SLOWLY, THE COTTON PLANTS
WILL GROW, GETTING TALLER AND TALLER WITH
THE HELP OF NATURE YOU KNOW.

THEN, ONE BY ONE THE COTTON PLANTS WILL BLOSSOM, PRODUCING A FIELD OF WHITE COTTON. THIS IS TOTALLY AWESOME.

THEN THE GROWER WILL HARVEST THE WHITE
FLUFFY FIELDS, SENDING LARGE BAGS OF THE
PICKED COTTON OFF TO THE MILLS.

THEY WILL MAKE T-SHIRTS AND DRESSES AND
PANTS AND GLOVES THERE. THEY WILL MAKE HATS,
SOCKS AND SNEAKERS, EVEN KIDS UNDERWEAR.

WEATHER ALSO EFFECTS THE THINGS THAT WE EAT.

I WILL SHOW YOU, LET ME SHOW YOU. THIS WILL BE A TREAT.

DO YOU LIKE CORN DOGS OR NACHOS OR THINGS THAT TASTE NEAT?

THEY COME FROM CORN... CORN... CORN...
CORN!

THE FARMER CAN PLANT CORN SEEDS OR
SMALLER CORN PLANTS TOO.
THEN WATCH NATURE TAKE OVER, IT KNOWS
WHAT TO DO.

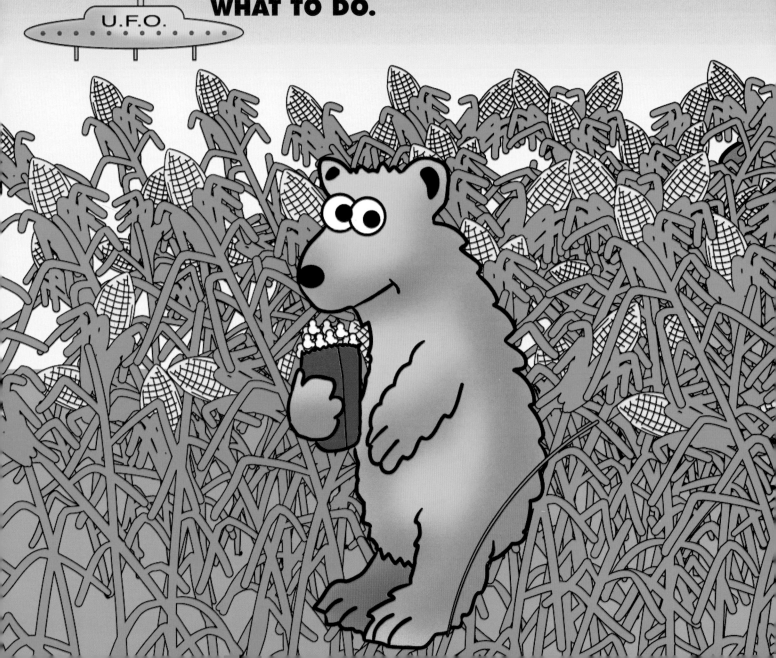

THERE IS PLENTY OF SUNSHINE. THAT IS WEATHER YOU KNOW. THEN THE PLANTS WILL GET WATER FROM FRESH RAIN OR SNOW.

THE CORN WILL GROW TALLER WITH MORE RAIN AND SUN. THEN TINY EARS OF CORN WILL GROW ONE BY ONE.

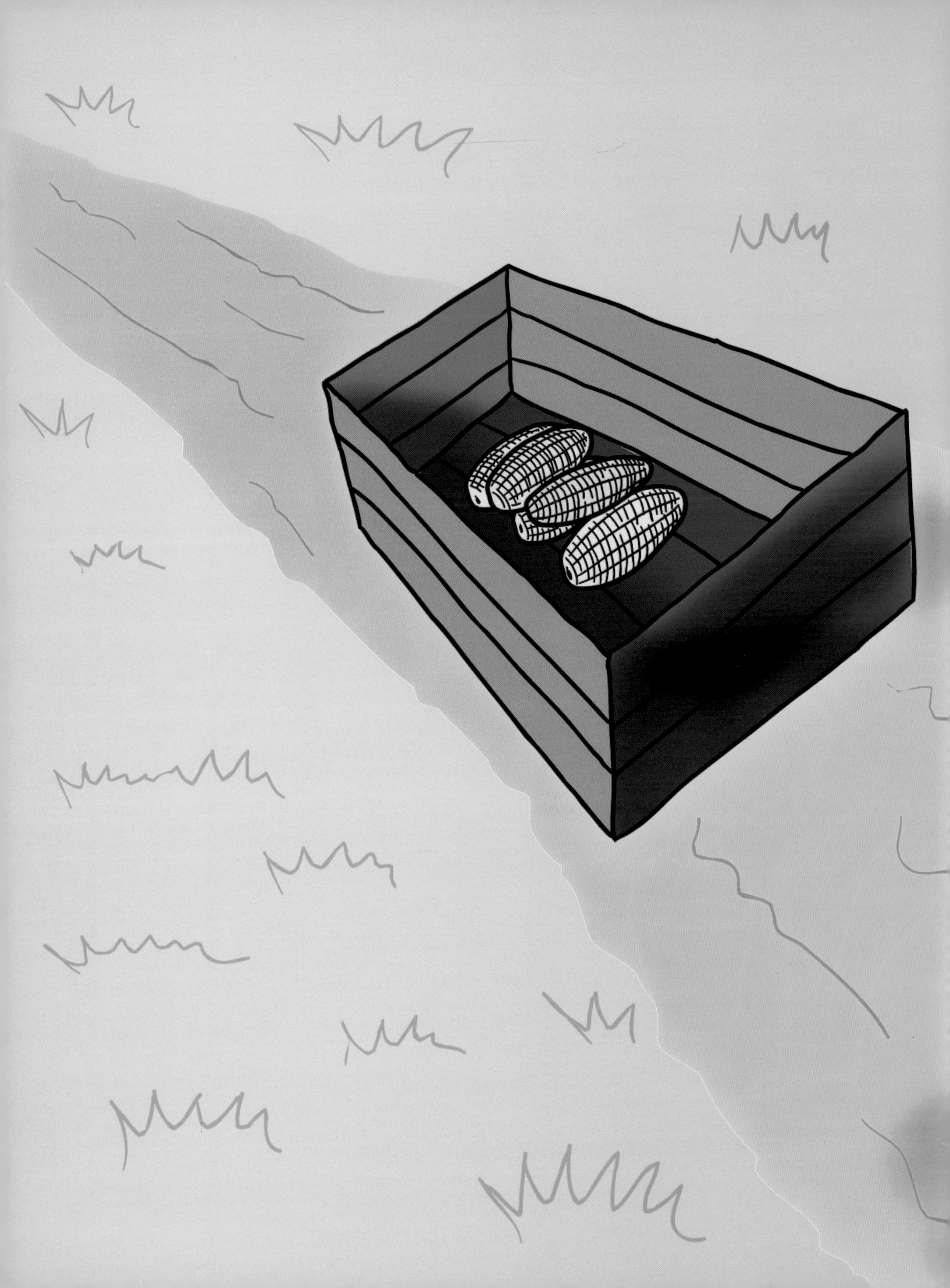

BOINK.. BOINK.. BOINK.. BOINK!

WHEN THE GROWING IS OVER, THE FARMERS WILL HARVEST. THERE WILL BE CORN TO FEED EVERYONE. WON'T THAT BE MARVELOUS?

CORN ON THE COB, CORNBREAD AND POPCORN TOO. FIELDS OF CORN, ACRES OF CORN FOR ME AND FOR YOU.

SOME CORN PRODUCTS WILL BE USED TO HELP OTHER PLANTS GROW. SOME CORN, SCIENTISTS WILL USE TO HELP YOUR HAIR SHINE AND GLOW.

SO YOU SEE HOW IMPORTANT WEATHER REALLY IS.
IT AFFECTS ONE AND ALL, NO MATTER WHERE WE LIVE.

IT HELPS GROW OUR FOOD THAT MAKES US GROW TALL. OR CAN KICK UP A WIND THAT CAN BLOW DOWN A WALL.

TAKE ONE SMALL ITEM AND I BET
WEATHER WILL PLAY A ROLE.

FROM THE HATS ON OUR HEADS TO
THE LEATHER ON OUR SHOE SOLES.

WEATHER EFFECTS EVERYTHING FOR YOUNG AND FOR OLD, NOW YOU KNOW WHY THE TITLE OF THIS BOOK IS SO BOLD.

IF NOT FOR WEATHER WE WOULD ALL BE NAKED. WAHBAHS DON'T MIND BUT CAN <u>YOU</u> TAKE IT?

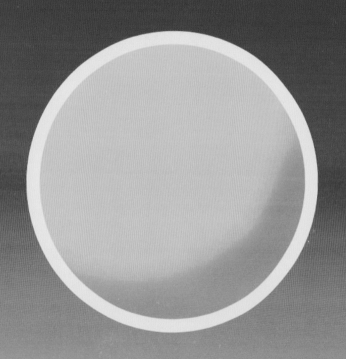

THE ENDS

HOW MANY OF MY BOOKS HAVE YOU ALREADY READ?

O   MUHAMMAD AND THE MARATHON
O   BEFORE THERE WERE PEOPLE
O   THE WEATHERMAN IS COMING TO MY SCHOOL TODAY
O   THE WEATHER PERSON'S HANDBOOK

BOOK ORDERS

To inquire about purchasing this book or any other books by Christopher Nance,
Call: **1 888 831-9268 (toll free).**

OR WRITE

Christopher Productions, Inc.
10153 ½ RIVERSIDE DRIVE, #266
TOLUCA LAKE, CALIFORNIA 91602

Call, write, or login on our web site, WWW.WEATHERDUDE.COM

We accept Visa, Master Card, Discover, or American Express - <u>PLEASE DO NOT
SEND CASH.</u>

You can make checks payable to **C.P.I. PUBLISHERS**

Returned checks are subject to the service charge for the greater of $15 or maximum
allowed by state law.

BOOK SIGNINGS

Please contact us at the above phone number or address if you are having a large book
fair at your school, church, or service organization and would like Christopher Nance to
attend for a book signing.

FAN CLUB & NEWSLETTER

If you would like to join Christopher Nance's fan club, "THE WEATHERDUDE", and
be included in our mailing list to receive a fun, free newsletter, send the following
information to our office address: **NAME, ADDRESS, AGE AND BIRTHDAY.**

VISIT US AT: WWW.WEATHERDUDE.COM